Going Inside

General Rahmatullah Safi, Peshawar August 22nd 1988

Going Inside

Memoir of an Afghan Holiday
with Rahmatullah Safi
1988

John England

GOING INSIDE

Published by ATSF 2016
Peterborough UK

Some names and identifying details have been changed to protect the privacy of
individuals.

Photography by John England
Cover photography by Andy Finney
Map of Afghanistan from CIA Fact Book (US Govt non-copyright)

To all those Afghans whose generosity, hospitality and kindness made my "holiday" such a memorable one

Preface

Rahmatullah Safi (just known as Safi) and his wife had been friends of mine since 1978.

That April my wife Shirley and I, both teachers, had moved from near Manchester, to Buckinghamshire. We decided we would try to buy a house in High Wycombe as this was one of the cheapest places to live in the area. One Saturday morning, an estate agent gave us the address of a house that was currently being rented but was also for sale.

We made our way to the property, an old three bed-roomed terrace, knocked on the door and it was answered quite quickly by a man with a very pronounced moustache. It was, as I was to find out later, Safi. We told him why we were there and he invited us in. He introduced us to his wife, and told us to have a look around. We did but it wasn't for us.

We made our way back to the lounge with the intention of thanking the couple and then leaving. In the lounge we were asked to sit on the settee and a general conversation ensued. We were given tea and invited to stay for lunch. Does that ever happen in any other home? Complete strangers being invited to stay for lunch? We made our excuses after about fifteen minutes and left.

We had both been impressed by the openness and generosity of the couple we had just met but thought that would be the first and the last time we saw them. How wrong we were.

A few months later, we put in a bid on a property that was very close to the house that we had visited that Saturday and after some nail-biting negotiations the house finally became ours.

From time to time we saw Safi, perhaps on the street, perhaps in the local shop and we told him where we now lived.

A few more months passed and one evening Safi was at the door. He was invited in and he then announced that they too had bought a house - on the opposite side of the street. We had become neighbours.

One night, Safi knocked on the door again. Could we help him with something called "references" for a job. We told him that these were usually concerned with the character or the ability of the person.

"Ah, ability, no problem," he said. "I did a training course with the SAS in Hereford in 1973. Also, I did a 'quick kill' course with U.S. Special Forces at Fort Bragg, North California. I have also undertaken some military training in the USSR. I did two courses, studying mountain and guerrilla warfare."

"Safi, I don't think these are the kind of references that you need for a job at a plastics factory. In fact I don't think you need to mention these at all. Having been in the army is sufficient."

"But I was a Colonel commanding Afghan Special Forces in the army of the King of Afghanistan."

Was this man having us on? Did he really believe that we would accept what he was saying was true?

Very gradually we found out that they were refugees from Afghanistan. His wife had been a lawyer in Kabul and Safi, indeed, had been a colonel in the Afghan army. So how was it that they were here in the UK in 1978?

In July 1973 Safi had returned to Afghanistan from Hereford where he had been on the training course with the SAS. A few weeks after his return the king, Zahir Shah, who was in Italy undergoing eye surgery at the time, was ousted in a coup. It was the king's cousin, Mohammed Daoud Khan who staged the coup. Khan then established a republican government.

Safi was jailed. After some months he escaped and went to Iran. From there he made his way to Rome where the king was in exile. He then came to the UK and was granted temporary admission status with a requirement to register with the police. In January 1978 Safi's wife and son arrived at Heathrow and were granted temporary admission pending a decision on their, and Safi's case.

The following month the family were granted refugee status and an extension of stay for a further year. Employment in the UK was not now restricted, though there was still a requirement to register with the police.

So, this was how they came to be living in High Wycombe and this was how both of them were trying to find work at a plastics factory. They were successful.

Rohulla, their son, aged seventeen, who spoke no English, started to attend college in Wycombe. He found it very difficult at first but with the help of some English friends was soon making spectacular progress and within three years had entered Manchester University to study chemical engineering.

Safi would often come round to our house. Once, he invited us to a barbeque. He was going to get some lamb, take it to West Wycombe Hill, a rather pleasant spot about a mile away, and cook it. It sounded great.

"The lamb might make a bit of noise but not much."

"Oh God Safi, I don't think that's a good idea! English people would not understand and they would not like you to do that there."

No barbeque, then.

One Sunday a very large black diplomatic car flying a small pendant arrived on our street. It was the Afghan ambassador from London visiting Safi.

In Afghanistan, in December 1979, Russian troops entered the country. In response to this The Islamic Unity of Afghanistan mujahideen was formed. This was also known as The Seven Party mujahideen Alliance or The Peshawar Seven. They were all Sunni Muslims.

One of the parties was The National Islamic Front of Afghanistan formed and led by Pir Sayeed Gailani. It was to this party that Safi later gave his allegiance.

In April 1982 the family was officially recognised as refugees and granted asylum in the UK. Now they could remain here permanently, change employment without permission from a government department and perhaps most importantly, if they left the UK they would normally be re-admitted at any time within two years of their departure by producing an official travel document. Also, they were no longer required to report to the police.

In 1983 Safi left for Peshawar and started to train the mujahideen. This included weapon, demolition and close quarter battle techniques.

In May 1983 we received a letter from Safi. His wife was now with him in Peshawar and trying to help out with the millions of Afghan refugees living in camps near to the city. Safi claimed that the Russian 38th Commando Brigade had been destroyed and that he was treating the captured prisoners of war – 150 soldiers and 11 officers – kindly. He also invited us to go and visit him in Pakistan.

Then came, in the same year, a letter from his wife. Safi was fighting in Afghanistan but she had got news of him from mujahideen returning to Peshawar from the fighting. He was well. She regretted that she was unable to teach in the refugee camps as the mullahs had decreed that there would be no girls' schools allowed there.

In November, Safi wrote whilst in Afghanistan. The weather was dreadfully cold but the mujahideen had inflicted great damage on the Russians, destroying four helicopters and two aircraft that were loaded with ammunition and explosives. However, presumably in retaliation, "Every day have been bombardments from 6.00am to 9.00pm ... fire just like hell."

In December 1983 there was another letter from Safi. His wife was back in Britain but by September 1984 she was back in Peshawar and bemoaning the fact that Safi had lost his address book so he had taken hers. All very well but he had been in Afghanistan with it for six weeks. She wrote ...

In August, a very important man came out from Afghanistan with three thousand people and destroyed all electric centres. There is not electricity in all Afghanistan.

A very brave pilot came from Afghanistan and brought an airplane with three communist officers. His family arrived five o'clock this morning.

One week ago Rahmat [Safi] captured two Russian soldiers. They are staying with us. Also they say they didn't like the Russian activities against Afghan people.

Four years passed and during that time we saw Safi when he returned to the UK to visit his family. Then, in June 1988 an invitation was received from Peshawar.

Dear John and Shirley,

I hope you are keeping well and I thank you for the letter. I am ok. I just come from Afghanistan. I hope you saw on ITN. [I think this was an interview with Sandy Gall inside Afghanistan.] This is 1.25 am 2-6-1988 and I am leaving to Afghanistan on 2.00am.

My driver and the body guards are asleep,
I don't mind. I can sleep in my jeep.

I will be so happy to see you in Peshawar
if you don't mind the heat.

I will take you any where you like and
I do my best to keep you happy.

If you make up your mind please let me know in advance, for some arrangements. Ask telephone from Rohulla and I see you in Islamabad and take you to Peshawar.

I am sorry I must ready for leave.

Your good friend

R Safi

I decided to go on an Afghan holiday.

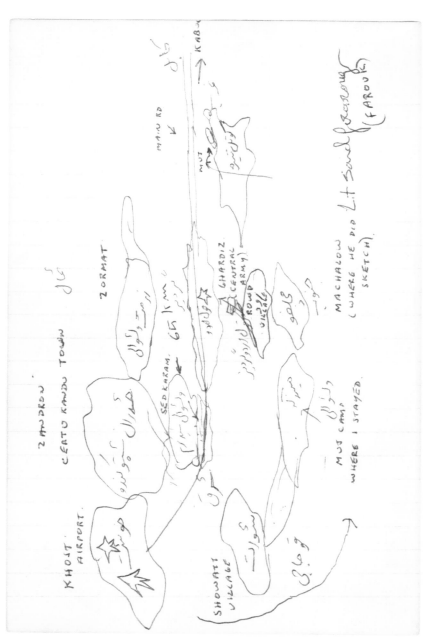

Hand drawn map of the area surrounding the city of Gardez, Afghanistan.

The Diary

Sunday July 31st 1988

I am due to fly to Islamabad from the UK and at the airport check-in desk I hand over my ticket and passport. The girl greets me in French. Why? I do not know.

"Flight 784 has been delayed until 10.30."

I mumble that I don't speak French very well. She replies, in English, "Your name is England and you can't speak French?"

What? What is she on about? Is this French humour?

On the plane I wonder what Rahmatullah Safi will do to while away the delay. I've brought him some pipe tobacco against the strict instructions of his wife, who now lives in London.

Monday August 1st

It's 08.10 and we've just touched down. It's much greener than I ever imagined with huge, brown rivers criss-crossing and meandering everywhere. I learn later that there are desperate floods in and around Islamabad and that it is the highest ever July rainfall.

Safi is waiting outside and we embrace warmly. He is a general in a mujahideen group fighting the Russians. I am a deputy head teacher of a primary school in England. We are good friends and he looks well if a little tired. He has his 'jeep', his bodyguard and driver, as promised.

Both of them have been with him for four years. I am greeted by the driver with both hands and "Salaam Aleikum."

We motor for about fifteen minutes and then enter a high class residential area where we stop for a few minutes. The bodyguard enters a house and soon returns with something in his arms. It is a Kalashnikov, an AK 47, a Russian sub-machine gun. I say nothing but now I know this trip is going to be very different.

The two and a half to three hour journey from Islamabad to Peshawar is exciting. My first impressions are of the huge convoys of multicoloured lorries all decked out with metal chains, then the bridges built by the British, and finally the Attock fort. This lies between the Peshawar road on one side and the River Indus on the other.

We stop for a meal: nan bread, chicken, mince beef savouries and to round it off a pint of freshly squeezed mango juice. It is delicious.

It's Monday afternoon and I am now in Safi's front garden in Peshawar, lying on the grass which is covered with a huge ground sheet and on top of that a type of green, khaki over-sheet. There are hard, large, red cushions and a spittoon. Standing a few feet away are two men. One is a Chinese looking servant who constantly serves up green tea with lemon juice and the other is Safi's personal bodyguard. He is about twenty two, a highly skilled fighter who has seen much action. In front of me is a tall, swarthy Afghan, about thirty five, sitting cross-legged. He is wearing grey 'Afghan' clothes and a dark green turban. To his right is an older man with a similar coloured turban and a two tone beard: white and black. Next to him is a giant of a man who has a fiercely strong handshake. These are commanders from the Jaji base in Afghanistan [See endnote 1].

Up to now there have been eight commanders come and go. One is an ex-member of the World Bank in Washington who has tried for the last ten years to build an alliance of the seven mujahideen groups fighting against the Russians. He is related to the famous commander Abdul Haq of Kabul who is a fundamentalist. Safi is trying to convert him!

More commanders arrive. One is from Nuristan which is located in the eastern part of the country.

This is how they arrive. One knocks at the large gate or rings a buzzer. A servant opens the door and informs Safi who it is. Safi nods and they are allowed to enter. A doctor and Safi's brigadier have just entered. The doctor speaks perfect English.

"Commanders come and go."

Usually they stay for ten to fifteen minutes and then leave. The commanders live nearby or in the many refugee/mujahideen camps in Peshawar.

Making some kind of sense of the conversation between Safi and the commanders is difficult and not just because of the language. I have gathered that they all belong to NIFA (the National Islamic Front of Afghanistan), a moderate party within the group of seven mujahideen parties opposed to the Russians. Members of NIFA come from different parts of the country and if there is a common thread it is that all of the people in Afghanistan should have a say in what kind of government there is to be after the war. Local leaders would be voted in by their tribe or village and then they would represent their constituents at a national assembly. The fundamentalist groups, I think, want a truly 'Muslim' state. "Culturally," Safi maintains, "we are all Muslims and proud of that but not to the extremes that groups like the Hesb-e Islami party led by Gulbuddin Hekmatyar [2] want us to go." NIFA is, perhaps, the most liberal of all the mujahideen groups and supports the return of King Zahir Khan [3] from exile in Rome. He was ousted in a coup in 1973.

Another servant has just given me my Afghan/Pak clothes. They are, of course, baggy grey cotton trousers and a large shirt or tunic of the same material and colour. The shirt is worn outside the trousers and is much longer than western shirts. They are commonly known as *shalwar kameez*. The servant shows me how to tie the trousers. I won't remember. I am also given a *pakol* by Safi. This is a soft, woollen, round topped hat and it becomes very important to me.

Safi introduces me to the boys. Three of them are from Kunduz, a city in northern Afghanistan. His bodyguard is called Desdegira. The boy who washes all the clothes is Mohammed. Abzel is his favourite. He loves him like a brother. He contracted malaria three months ago and before that he had suffered a horrible wound to his arm and Safi had sent him to Switzerland to have it put back together. One of the servants has lost two brothers in the war and another was a "bastard." Why did he say this? Because he too (Safi) was a bastard – part evil. I laugh but Safi maintains that all Pathans [4] have a fighting streak in them even in peace time. It is in their nature. Certain tribes are fighting for the Russians and being repaid with money and food. Presumably they are bastards too.

"His bodyguard is called Desdegira."

In the back garden a horse is tethered and it is, I am informed, related to the king's horse. It is Safi's pride and joy. Also, there are two very fierce dogs tied up to two trees. God help me if they get loose. There are two sentries. One is at the front gate and the other in the back garden. They are both in wooden structures which overlook the high wall surrounding the property. Why are they there? To protect Safi from the

Going Inside

KGB [5] and Fundamentalists. He says he has had assassination notes sent to the house. What world have I entered?

Supper is lamb, beef, rice and courgettes with melon to follow. Delicious.

At nine Safi is listening to the BBC World Service and says there has been an explosion in north London. After, he takes me to my room and shows me two Kalashnikovs which are under my bed. He then gives me a pistol. This is really, really strange. I wouldn't know what to do with them. I've never handled such things in my life.

" Supper is lamb, beef, rice and courgettes."

Tuesday August 2nd

I awake at 04.45 and am writing this under my mosquito net. There is a large fan whirring round from the ceiling and there is air conditioning if I want it. The room, about twelve by twelve feet, is covered by three large Afghan rugs. There is a television and video, a large radio-cassette recorder, an electric fire for winter and a desk which is covered with photos and letters. The shower room is straight ahead and has a hand basin and toilet.

Breakfast is a white cheese formed like a large cake, nan bread, honey and Peshawar biscuits. This is washed down by numerous cups of green tea. I love it with freshly squeezed lemon. The morning paper, the English edition of *The Muslim*, has been delivered. It is cloudy today and a gentle rain is falling when I first get up. In the back garden which is rectangular and measures roughly 25 by 14 metres I have just taken two pictures. One is of Safi's horse and the other is of the two ferocious dogs who seem to sleep during the day. However, just as I am about to snap them, up they get, barking and pulling at their chains.

I read the paper and then part of Doris Lessing's book *The Wind Blows Away Our Words*. It is good on atmosphere but a little simplistic in analysis.

Safi arrives back from a meeting at about twelve and asks if I want to see "action" or just walk in the north of Afghanistan. In any event I have to go inside Afghanistan "properly." This means that I should not be "discovered" by the Pakistani authorities. If I am I'll be put in prison. Journalists take their own chances! Legally, I am not even supposed to leave Peshawar. I don't know how to feel. I tell him I want to see the country but that I don't want to put him or his men in danger. He shrugs his shoulders and says we'll go for a little walk outside. Desdegira is with us.

After about five minutes we arrive at a tiny, open fronted room where young tailors are at work. These children are the ones who have made alterations to my Afghan clothes. After a drink at another small shop we return home passing some children playing in a river. Lunch is served outside on the grass. Almost immediately the buzzer goes and two mujahideen are allowed in. I am told later that one of them has shot down two aircraft with stinger missiles whilst in action near Herat, western Afghanistan. Is this true? I have no idea. The commander from

"These children are the ones who have made alterations to my Afghan clothes."

Khost [6] and the director of intelligence arrive. Desdegira appears and shakes the hands of the two mujahideen and Safi shouts at him for not showing respect to the officers first. I am told that we are going inside tomorrow, to Paktia province, south of Kabul. Also, I must learn how to handle weapons and that Safi will show me on the lawn tonight.

What can I say? I suppose that if I have to I will use them but I don't want to. I have no military training, no army background and I have never held a gun let alone fired one. I lie. I used one once at a fairground.

Wednesday August 3rd

I am woken at 03.45 and told to be ready for 04.00. I have already packed: medicines, toilet rolls, socks, underpants, towel, camera and films, passport and money in a small rucksack.

Between Peshawar and Tarimangal at the Afghan border, there must have been thirty to forty Pakistan army posts. Some have a barrier across the road whilst others have just one or two men on either side of the road. Safi sits in the front of his military style jeep: pipe, sunglasses, upright bearing, a military man, every bit a general. Me in the back in my *shalwar kameez*, *pakol* and trainers. I have been instructed to wear these rather than my walking boots.

At each check point I am told to look at Desdegira who is opposite me giving the impression I am listening to what he is saying. If I am caught at one of the checkpoints I will be put in prison for a few days and then deported. This is not a joke but I am not scared or frightened.

We are stopped twice, once just outside Peshawar at the first post and then much later on. Safi's bluff, if needed, is to produce a signed picture of General Zia, the President of Pakistan. He does give the impression of being a general in the Pakistani army.

We go through Dara Adam Khel, Kohat, Hangu, Doaba, Thal and at 09.30 stop at a NIFA ammunition base and training camp. The road leading to it is extremely poor and very bumpy. I am shaky and terribly thirsty. The old camp leader there asks me if I want tea and very shortly English tea is served with milk, in a bone china tea service that could have graced the Queen's table but before I can drink I have to be sick. When I return I am asked if I am alright and offered fried eggs, honey and nan. I refuse but I want to drink more and must have seven or eight cups of tea. I feel much better but then I have to go the toilet. Diarrhoea!

After leaving, we go through Parachinar and finally arrive at Tarimangal. This border town has taken a real hammering but even though it's officially in Pakistan the mujahideen flag still flies and it is packed with heavily armed men.

From here there is a semi-road leading up a mountain and I think that no vehicle can get up there but the jeep does – climbing, climbing, climbing until – AFGHANISTAN. We reach Jaji. I have just heard my first gunfire: rat tat tat tat, loud and a little frightening. I think it must be the muj having some firing practice.

"English tea is served with milk."

"We reach Jaji."

Going Inside

"There is artillery all around…"

Going Inside

"…and small children from about five upwards."

"The men start singing and dancing."

The camp is amazing. You enter the valley and on each side there are steep embankments covered with pine trees. There are dugouts, small mud and stone bungalows extending far up the valley. We go for a walk to the furthest sentry outposts and I imagine it is good for morale that Safi goes and has a few words with the men. There is artillery all around and small children from about five upwards. The men are in their early twenties and thirties. No women.

Supper is meat, rice, huge pieces of nan bread and melon and afterwards something amazing happens. The men start singing and dancing. To me this is significant because I don't think fundamentalists sing and dance. I sleep on the floor in the dining room.

Thursday August 4th

"We are in the lead jeep."

We leave the camp at 08.30 and move into Afghanistan. We are in the lead jeep and the local commanders and some fighters in another two. At first the countryside is barren as all the crops have been destroyed and there are huge numbers of bombed buildings. We pass through a garrison town evacuated by the Russians a few months earlier. Everywhere are the remains of Russian tanks, lorries and armoured vehicles.

"Huge numbers of bombed buildings."

Going Inside

"Everywhere are the remains of Russian tanks, lorries and armoured vehicles."

"The roads are mainly huge holes or river beds."

Going Inside

Eventually the landscape changes and there are fertile valleys, presumably the Russians need the local produce. Past Alikhel, past Narai the scene of fierce fighting and on to Ahmadkhel. I have visions of mines and Russian MiG fighter planes and other nasties. However Safi says the road is clear and that it is controlled by the muj. It is.

The jeeps are fantastic as the roads are mainly huge holes or river beds. Often we have to go through quite deep rivers with the waves preceeding us. All around are huge numbers of brightly coloured flags indicating where mujahideen have died. Eventually, after getting bogged down once or twice, we make our way along a plain and I am told that a Norwegian lady has died in an explosion here a few days previously. A road mine. I assume she was a journalist.

"Eventually…we make our way along a plain."

"We have a puncture."

We have a puncture and I am informed that when we stop and get out, not to stray from the road. The wheel is replaced and at Kalkeen we have the puncture repaired. There is a large muj cemetery here and I see two women in colourful clothes. As soon as they see me they turn their backs and draw up their veils. I am told by Safi that the village leader has recently asked if they could join NIFA. "I told them to fuck off. They have remained neutral up till now but judgement day is near, the Russians are withdrawing and they want to go with the winners. There will be retribution." I say that this is harsh on people but he argues that many of the villagers here went to the refugee camps in Peshawar and that the remaining people here had to make clear choices: for or against.

We must have been there for about forty five minutes when a large Russian truck filled with muj arrives. It is on the way to Gardez. One of the fighters, about twenty years old, speaks good English and he tells me he has been a student in Peshawar. Many of the men, there must be twenty to thirty, want their picture taken and as they are driving off they shout out their devotion to both Allah and Safi. It is quite moving. Very shortly after that, we follow them and Safi and I talk about the nature of responsibility and how lonely it can be.

Going Inside

"There is a large muj cemetery here."

Going Inside   29

"Many of the men…want their picture taken."

Going Inside

"As they are driving off they shout out their devotion to both Allah and Safi."

Going Inside

"We are invited into an old man's house."

Eventually we come to Mirzaka and stop in the road and can't go on because the Russian artillery is five to six kilometres away and we could easily be spotted. Indeed, we hear shells exploding about a kilometre away. The decision is taken to wait until sunset before moving out. We are invited into an old man's house. It has one room. There is a bed, a few rugs on the floor and some cushions up against a wall. A gun hangs on the opposite wall. The man invites us to stay for supper and he sends out to the next village for a chicken. There are none. I am amazed at the kindness and the generosity of this very poor man. We are plied with tea, of course, and I am told to lie on the bed. I sleep.

At sunset we depart but before we do all the men pray. I don't know why but I am not scared or frightened. I should be, but I feel safe. At this point you can see quite well with a visibility of perhaps one hundred metres. No smoking is allowed and Safi plays Afghan music on the car cassette. Crazy! There are no headlights, no lights at all.

We go on slowly and it is becoming darker and darker and I am a little nervous now. Are there mines? I will have no chance of survival out here. Safi says it's possible that some spy has got a message through that he is arriving. Why is he saying this? After 15 to 20 minutes we turn right at Alamgai onto another track. We are five kilometres from the Russian guns. This sounds a lot but earlier that afternoon I had seen the shell smoke more than a kilometre behind where we were with the old man. By now it is pitch dark and I can see no more than two to three metres in front. God knows how the driver is managing. We pass Machlagho and Said Karam, near the ancestral village of Najibullah, the Afghan President [7].

Finally we arrive near the mujahideen camp. We don't enter and Safi tells the guards to notify the commander that he has arrived. It is total darkness except for the brilliant light of the stars. All around we can see red flashes and hear loud explosions. Safi and the others begin to pray. Then the sound of planes – two distinct sounds.

I am told later that one is the spotter plane taking infrared photographs. Then when it discovers where the muj positions are the fighter jet or jets would come. There are flares being dropped but I don't know how far away. We wait for about an hour and a half and I am both calm and excited. It's a strange feeling. A tractor goes past, without lights, taking ammunition to the fighters and there are sentries moving around sometimes blowing whistles. I am told not to speak English loudly. Why? Because there could be fundamentalist mujahideen around. A British photographer had been killed by such a group [8].

Eventually a message is received that the local commander has arrived back and we leave in the jeep to meet him. Soon we enter a courtyard and then a large room. The time is 00.20 and this is the scene. We are a little underground and the room is about 20 feet by 12. All around the walls muj are sitting cross-legged or with one knee on the floor and one leg behind. There are sixteen men some in brilliant white or dark green turbans. One man sitting in the centre of the room is holding forth. Everybody listens. Tea is constantly being served from old fashioned teapots. The walls are bare and there are two small niches adjacent to the entrance where shoes are put. The only man carrying a gun is Desdegira, Safi's bodyguard, though the man next to him, commander Alozai, is wearing an ammunition belt that goes around his neck and under his shoulder.

Next to me is the commander I first met in Peshawar. I think his name is Gullab but it might be Wazir. There is no electricity and the only light is a paraffin hurricane lamp. I can't see most of the men opposite but one points at me and shows his club foot. I think he must be angry with me for writing but he is not. He got his club foot fighting,

"Sitting cross-legged or with one knee on the floor and one leg behind."

he says, for the true meaning of Islam not that practised by the fundamentalists like Khomeni. Ayatollah Khomeni, a Shia Muslim, is an Iranian religious and political leader.

Much of the discussion, I later learn, is precisely about this – the true meaning of Islam. Soon club foot makes all the others laugh. He insults the Mangal tribe (these are Pashtuns living in Paktia province) saying that they are arrogant, as they believe they are next to the Prophet. While everyone else strives to reach the ladder of perfection by praying, the Mangals pray just once. Their words are, "Thank you God for making ME close to the Prophet."

Most use the spittoon and the louder and longer the spit the better. Some have Afghan snuff or is it *khat* which they put in their mouths, chew and then spit out.

Friday August 5th

I awake at 05.30 and take my small rucksack to go for a wash. I haven't shaved since leaving Peshawar and I must stink. No more than usual. I have been badly bitten on one of my legs but my arms and face which have been smeared with 'jungle formula' seem to be unaffected. It might be fleas rather than mosquitoes. I don't care as they aren't really bothering me. I have to go to the toilet and there is no toilet but open ground. I take down my baggy trousers, then my underpants and haul up the tunic with my left hand and I do the business. It is light brown and not too soft. That's good. Mind you, undoing the baggy trousers I nearly loose the cord going inside the band. I can just imagine me holding up my trousers for the rest of my stay.

Last night, before going to sleep, I went for a wee in the courtyard. It was pitch black. Suddenly a black heap jumped up. I thought, oh God I have pissed on a muj sleeping outside. It was a goat. After washing, I ask Safi if I can take some photos. Yes but no photos of women. I haven't seen any women!

"I haven't seen any women!"

"Some of the men leave for the fighting."

I can hear guns firing and the club foot commander from last night shows me where there is to be a battle. He points three or four kilometres away to the city of Gardez which is the capital of Paktia Province.

"Escorted by four bodyguards and the commander with the club foot who is now on a horse."

Going Inside

"I am sitting on the balcony of the safe house."

It has, I am told, up to fifteen thousand Russian troops and is of great strategic importance. The city of Khost is nearby.

At breakfast I am informed that I am not to go to the front line and some of the men leave for the fighting. There is already loud gun firing. Instead, I am to be taken to a safe house escorted by four body-guards and the commander with the club foot who is now on a horse. We walk for about a mile and one of the muj wants to photograph me. I am writing all this as I am sitting on the balcony of the safe house looking at a fantastic rug. It is about fifteen feet long with blue and green diamond shapes on a dark blue background. I feel completely safe. It's 08.30. I wonder about home and my wife. Shirley, has the telephone line been installed? Are you still sleeping in your warm bed? Are you looking forward to going to Paris with Joan?

We are completely surrounded by trees but the sun is shining through strongly. Guns are firing. Boom – Boom. I can hear planes in the sky. I was told last night that Gardez was going to be attacked today with a sophisticated weapon. God only knows what that means.

Going Inside

"I am taken…to observe the battle."

One of the bodyguards is drawing me a map of where we are in relation to Gardez. I show them my passport and the visa for Pakistan. They laugh. They have no concept about a passport. Then I produce the medicines I have brought with me and try and act out what each is for: anti malaria tablets, tablets for diarrhoea, antiseptic cream, sterotabs that I haven't used, 'jungle formula', after bite cream and toilet rolls. Toilet rolls get a really good laugh as they wipe their bottoms with dried mud. Paper for wiping your bottom indeed!

I haven't been ill since that day we left Peshawar and I feel well and in good health.

Soon, I am taken by the four of them to a small hill a quarter of a mile away to observe the battle. In the mountains to my left are muj artillery firing onto Russian tank and gun positions just outside the city. To the north there are other muj fighters.

The first thing you see is the smoke on the Russian positions where the muj shells have landed. From the Russian side you see the flash of rockets and then soon after the explosions in the mountains. A muj arrives on his horse and he is a forward observer for the fighters. By means of a walkie talkie, a hand-held, portable, two way radio transmitter, he points out if the shells are on target or too long or short.

Going Inside

"The first thing you see is the smoke on the Russian positions."

There is much joking and laughing and each time there is smoke I am urged on to take photos. I feel perfectly safe.

"He is a forward observer for the fighters."

Going Inside

"We are sitting on the balcony waiting for dinner."

It's 11.20 and Safi has just returned from the front line. We are waiting now for the retribution – the air attacks on the mujahideen positions. The commander with the club foot has just told a sentry not to get too close to us but to watch from a greater distance. Safi translates this a little differently.

"Fuck off you motherfucker and keep guard. There may be spies around."

We are sitting on the balcony waiting for dinner. There is the club foot commander, a brigadier named Azeemullah, Desdegira of course, the two commanders who came from Peshawar and a scribe who is writing continuously. The club foot and Safi are in private session but eventually Safi comes over and tells me we are leaving tonight when the moon rises and going back the same way as we came in. We may stay in the village where the old man lives as Safi is going to meet the leaders of the local tribes. What that's about? I don't know yet. He ends by saying that the Russians would like to capture two VIPs. "They are not too happy with me."

During the afternoon I ask if I can walk into the orchard which is not far away and I am told that it's okay if I have a bodyguard. There, two muj kill a goat, hang it from a tree and skin it.

"I ask if I can walk into the orchard."

"Two muj kill a goat, hang it from a tree and skin it.."

Going Inside

Back on the balcony everyone is sitting around drinking tea and we have to hang around because we can't leave until dark. The radio is on and the channel is changed and then … "It's a hundred and twenty six for five. Logie caught Gooch bowled Foster who now has five wickets." Foster's next ball is a wide – the first of the match.

Here I am at a battle front listening to a test match from the Oval. I laugh out loud at the total absurdity of the situation and two commanders laugh too though I'm sure they don't know why.

By 19.45 it's getting dark and I know that soon I will be leaving. I look around and wonder at the rugs, the trays of tea, the guns, the ammunition, the hand held grenade or mortar launcher and the men.

Supper is served at 20.30. Huge nan, rice and the goat I saw earlier. Cooked, it is brought in huge pieces and taken from a large bucket with a long, two pronged fork and then put in front of you. It's like having a whole chicken. Now I like meat but I don't like fat on meat and this huge piece in front of me is almost pure fat, or so it seems to me. I eat the bread, a few vegetables and a tiny, tiny piece of the fat. I nearly gag and I try and speak to Safi but he is in deep conversation with someone else. Then I see the man who has given me the goat from the bucket return. He spears my almost untouched meat, puts it into the bucket and then delivers an even bigger piece. I am mortified. They are all looking at me. I interrupt Safi and tell him that I can't eat the goat: it's too fatty. He's smiling and laughing and I hate him for this. He says this goat has been killed in our honour and that they don't eat like this often. I have been given a bigger piece of goat because it is obvious I am displeased with the initial portion. My humiliation is complete.

"Please explain to them that this is not true," I plead. Safi starts talking to the group – about ten of us and soon there is laughter and the conversation resumes. I don't know what Safi has said. It could have been some totally rude comment about me but I don't care. When the meal is finished I ask Safi to thank the local Gardez mujahideen for being so hospitable. Safi does so and then the club foot commander speaks and Safi translates. He says that I when I get back to London I should tell the BBC that what they want is a moderate form of Islam, that we are all Muslims but we are not all fundamentalists. I am humbled when he thanks me for coming and being his guest. I reply that I am sorry that the West has not given them much help. There are three million refugees, many of them in and around Peshawar.

Saturday August 6th

We leave at 01.00 and there is a crescent moon. I am a little scared this time as I have heard and seen the guns this morning. There are three vehicles, two jeeps and a Toyota pick up. Once again no lights, everyone quiet, no smoking. There are all sorts of weapons on board.

It takes us two hours to reach the safety of the old man's house but we keep travelling and stop at Kalkeen for a few minutes and then arrive at Ahmadkhel where we climb a small hill to get to a house. Here I fall asleep for a few minutes as do the others. Soon tea, honey and nan bread is served. I understand now when Safi says he's tired.

We move on and soon, some muj leave us to go to the ammunition camp and a picture is taken of me on top of another abandoned tank. As I am getting down from the tank, on the opposite side to where I got on, my vanity is rewarded – a ferocious dog snarls, growls and leaps at me. I run and run and, thank God, it is tethered under the tank with a large chain. I am met with howls of laughter from the muj.

"Me on top of another abandoned tank."

"Camels carrying ammunition shells."

On we go and out of the blue, at around 04.30, Safi wants to know if I would like to walk in the Kunar mountains which are in the north -east of Afghanistan and are the highest in the country. They take three days to climb I am told. I don't think so!

We reach Jaji at 10.55 and I am exhausted and sleep but am woken for dinner at 12.30. Over food, Safi tells me that some Shia leader was murdered yesterday and that we must leave for Peshawar soon, other-wise the roads will be closed. I don't ask why because I'm too tired but I know this journey. It is evil.

On the way down the mountain from Jaji we see camels carrying ammunition shells for the muj. Like coming, we have to pass through many Pakistani army posts but we are not troubled. Whilst buses and trucks are stopped we just keep going. Safi puts on his sun glasses and looks every inch a Pakistani general. Once, as we approach a post with a soldier in the middle of the road waving us down, Safi shouts at a snoring Desdegira because he is slow in putting on the inside light that shows we are a military jeep carrying a general. However, as soon as the soldier recognises the jeep and particularly the armed bodyguard he waves us on.

Going Inside

Our driver, who has been behind the wheel for the whole journey is magnificent. He chews khat and I suppose this helps him to keep awake. There are cows and donkeys in the middle of the road and people sitting at the side. He hits the horn the whole time and there are many uses for it. It warns the car in front you are overtaking, it warns people crossing the road to get out of the way and it warns cars on the other side of the road not to overtake. Back home there would be an awful lot of anger and swearing by those being 'horned'. This is not the case here. Passivity is the order of the day.

We stop twice for prayers and I ask Safi what his attitude to prayers is. "What is most important" he says "is your heart, your attitude to your fellow man." That ties in with my own belief that if there is a God then God will not be bothered if you are a Christian, Muslim, Jew, Hindu or nothing at all. What God might be concerned about is how you treat your fellow man. Fine, but what about the fighting?

"Our driver."

Sunday August 7th

It is now 11.00 and we are back in Peshawar, after a twenty hour journey, and I am refreshed by a long sleep and a wonderful shower in the garden where I was 'hosepiped' down. My clothes have been hand washed by Mohamed and I feel a new man. When I was 'inside' I never had a proper wash, just a splash on the face and feet. No shower, no deodorant, no shave.

Desdegira has given me some *khat* to chew and I am finishing a letter to Shirley, my wife, and after addressing the envelope Safi tells a servant to post it. I give the boy a 100 rupee note. Safi says no and returns the note to me. I insist and give the note to the boy again. Safi tells me to sit down and listen. I shout at him and tell him to listen to me.

"I have been given everything by you: food, drink, clothing, transportation, petrol and that's just here. 'Inside' everything was provided again. I haven't spent a rupee since I've been here. I feel bad that I am not being allowed to contribute anything. I insist that I contribute."

Safi has been listening and then he smiles, laughs loudly and says, "Now you listen to me." He then talks about the Afghan Muslim way of treating guests, of how even if an unknown but invited family lived in his house for three years he would provide. I feel guilty at this wondering how I would react if the same thing happened at home. No chance of two weeks!

Safi then goes onto say how the old man tried to get a chicken for him to eat even though he was very poor, how the muj killed a goat for him even though they do not eat like that normally. He accepts these offerings but he remembers them. Then, when he can he will reciprocate – in triplicate.

Today is a lazy day and I eat, rest, sleep and talk. In the garden all the equipment is being made ready for the trip to Kunar. We go on Thursday but not to do too strenuous a climb. Safi says I am here for a holiday and not for such hard work. At six we go to Peshawar and I take my films to be developed. I remind Safi that I want to buy some rugs and he says he will get his friend to look into it. Things are never simple!

Going Inside

Mon August 8th

At 05.30 we go for a ten mile drive to a local butcher, just as you do early on a Monday morning. He did not have a shop but a table outside and whilst the meat is being prepared I have a glass of tea. A man approaches me and shakes my hand. He is a mullah and apparently he tells Safi to try and convert me. Safi could be making it up for all I know. On the way home a large crowd is gathered at the side of the road. Two Afghan refugee children who had been collecting scrap metal had got hold of an unexploded bomb which had gone off. Both were killed.

Back home we discuss the conflict and how it may end. There are so many factors to be considered.

1   Russia does not want the Fundamentalists
     in power over the whole of Afghanistan. That
     would put pressure on their border.
2   The country may well split into two or three. In
     the North, perhaps, centred on the city of Mazar-
     i-Sharif, a communist sphere of influence. In
     the South, a fundamentalist regime under the
     protection of Pakistan and President General Zia.
3   The seven mujahideen groups come to their own
     arrangements under a plan worked out by the UN
     where the people have a direct say in what goes on.
4   The Russians leave and then make propaganda
     saying that the Afghans can't control their own
     affairs because of the resulting civil war.

It is difficult to know what will happen. However, Safi says that an interim government has been pencilled in for when the Russians leave and that he has been asked to become Minister of Defence. He has turned it down. He has sacrificed many members of his family. His father he couldn't recognise because he had been blown to pieces. His brother died in a Soviet prison. He wants to retire and enjoy the rest of his life.

The buzzer goes, the door is opened and in comes Safi's scribe from the safe house at Gardez and a commander from the area around

Khost which is also quite close to Gardez. Apparently there are to be joint operations with different mujahideen groups but one commander doesn't want to know. Safi is to sort the problem out and this is an order from the leader and founder of NIFA, Pir Sayeed Gailani [9].

Soon, three commanders and the dissident arrive. They are from the Hesb-i-Islami (Khalis) led by Mohammed Yunis Khalis [10]. One of them is the brother of Abdul Haq commander at the capital, Kabul. He has met Mrs Thatcher in London. One of the others has a brother in law also living in London. He asks me, after they have spoken to Safi, why Britain won't take any refugees. What can I say?

"I change sixty pounds."

Tuesday August 9th

I am up early, as usual, and after breakfast a young English speaking member of NIFA who works for Safi in the security section arrives. His name is Kamardin and he has been told to take me around Peshawar. Outside he hails a tuk-tuk, a motor rickshaw with three wheels. It is usually used for travelling short distances within cities.

Our first stop is at the black market to change travellers' cheques and the man there offers me twenty nine rupees to the pound. I am a little hesitant as the paper gives an exchange of thirty. However, I am not going to quibble over one rupee and I change sixty pounds.

"There are hundreds of bracelets, earrings, bangles…"

I am after lapis lazuli and am taken to an old antique shop in a tiny alleyway. There are hundreds of bracelets, earrings, bangles, necklaces and copper mugs. I am given tea and I make my choice – a few rings, two bangles, a pair of earrings and a necklace. The interpreter does the business and I pay 1100 rupees, about thirty six pounds. A bargain, who knows? I certainly don't. We leave and I suggest a drink.

Going Inside

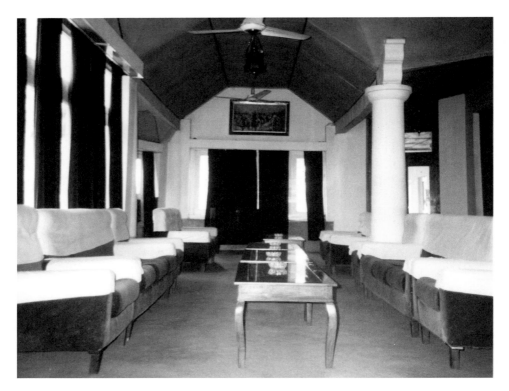

"Dean's Hotel…really is a remarkable place"

He takes me to Dean's Hotel [11] and it really is a remarkable place. There are green settees and large armchairs covered, on the arms and head, with white cotton covers. Two fans are whirring out their tune and there is an air conditioning machine. Directly opposite me are glass covered wooden tables and a picture of Afghan warriors on horses. There is even a fireplace here. Behind me is the bar. I am still alcohol-free and my liver must be nearly fully restored. I tend to smoke more, though.

Afterwards, the bazaar is fantastic: small alleys with a large variety of small dark rooms. There are tailors, gun makers and sellers, butchers and watch repairers. I want my watch strap repaired and there's no charge except for a cigarette. Very young boys weave in tiny workshops. There is a specific area for the butchers and it is both fascinating and horrific. A cow is lead off the road and its head is forced to the ground. The neck is placed over a large drainage hole and cut. The animal makes no sound. The butchers can now get to work. Near here I see the first 'Westerners.' I am invisible to them in my 'Afghan' clothes.

"Small alleys with a large variety of small dark rooms."

Going Inside

"Very young boys weave in tiny workshops."

"I am invisible to them in my 'Afghan' clothes"

This afternoon I watch videos of the fighting and doze. The heat drains me and I am constantly sweating. I drink tea to replace the loss.

At six we leave in the jeep and make our way to Munda refugee camp about twenty miles from Peshawar. We are taking one of the commanders from Kabul to see his brother there. Many of the refugees have been here for ten years and most are nominal members of one of the seven muj groups. The Pakistani authorities require them to register with a party to receive a food ration card.

The camp itself is depressing but as we are gathered around a fire Safi recognises one of the old men there and later, back in Peshawar, tells a story. The old man's father was a compulsive thief and had been so for many years. Safi's father finally caught him and said to the man that if he would swear on the Holy Koran not to steal again he would make sure that the governor of the province gave him a pardon. The man did so. However he was such a compulsive thief that he used to take half of his belongings to his uncle's house and when it was dark he came and stole his own possessions in order to keep his hand in! The story amused everyone.

I have a pack of cards and I teach four of the boys whist. They love it. However three of them get very annoyed when one starts cheating. He doesn't follow suit when he can. Safi laughs and surprises me when he calls Desdegira over and talks to him. After a short while Desdegira gives a reply. Safi has asked him how much money it would take for Desdegira to kill him. An awful lot is the reply. Both of them laugh and I am left wondering if this is a joke or not. Given that various tribes, in Afghanistan, swap allegiances very readily I don't know. Safi tells me that Afghans are natural fighters. They don't need training as they use guns in their everyday life. After the war, with all the extra guns they have acquired, life in the villages will go on as normal – that is fighting each other.

Wednesday August 10th

Safi announces this morning that he has to go inside tonight, to Khost. There is a dispute between two commanders of different tribes but that he won't be away for long. He says it is too difficult to smuggle me in. I am, of course, disappointed and wish I was going. I am told that Kamerdin will come and take me out.

I read Peter Levi's book *The Light Garden of the Angel King: Travels in Afghanistan*. I find out that Nuristan, a province in the eastern part of Afghanistan, was formerly known as Kafiristan: the land of the infidels. Also, I listen to the BBC World Service. President Najibullah meets with political and religious leaders in Kabul. I can't really see him lasting long when the Russians leave.

Safi returns from the muj training camp at 14.00 and his shoulder shows the signs of rifle recoil.

"Didn't that boy come and take you out? The miserable bastard." He shouts this out. I laugh.

Before Safi and Abzel leave I am shown a gun. It is a P-4074 sniper rifle. I think it is American.

Abzel oils all the mechanisms but first he washes all the bits in turpentine. He is quite meticulous about it.

Nayeem puts a thin piece of rope down the barrel of the gun. Attached to the end of the rope is a piece of rag which is soaked in oil. The bullets must be three to four inches long.

Going Inside

Thursday August 11th

Sekander wakes me with the immortal words, "Chai, chai!" I must be an addict by now. I take a book off the shelf and it is the autobiography of Armand Hammer, an American oil magnate. Of course, inside the front cover: *With my best wishes Armand Hammer Sept 1987*. I am told later that when Safi is in America giving a television interview he receives a message from Hammer who wants to meet him and his personal jet is sent to bring him to Los Angeles. The most important part of the story though was when he went to meet Hammer at his office. There were plenty of sexy secretaries and he wished he was twenty five again. Soon afterwards Hammer takes Safi to Rome to see the exiled king. Pure Holywood!

Safi is honoured in San Francisco. They awarded him the freedom of the city. A large, gold coloured key is in the bedroom.

I am asked by Abdul, by means of sign language, if I have any washing and I give him some shorts, underwear and a t-shirt. It's wonderful having everything clean after going inside. I wonder about Safi as he left at 03.30 last night.

Kamerdin doesn't come but after lunch I am allowed into Peshawar with Nayeem. We take the tuk tuk to Sarafa bazaar where I change fifty dollars on the black market and get nineteen to the dollar. The bank's rate is seventeen. I need a week to walk around here properly but I am much more confident and recognise certain places. We have tea in Green's [11] and I can tell this is another world for Nayeem. He keeps staring, looking around and making sure that when I take a sip of tea he does too.

When we get back, Kamerdin is there and he apologises for not coming in the morning. He is very busy at work. Two commanders are let in and I am asked if people in Britain put money on cards. Can you get melon and green tea? Are there boarding schools? Do I have any children?

Later on I take a picture of the servants sleeping. In their room, on the walls are some pictures of beautiful women taken from the covers of Woman's Weekly. 1950s I'd say.

Friday August 12th

I go into the garden and the dogs are loose. I have a huge fright and rush back inside. One of them has a bloodied ear and it's obvious it's been bitten by the other dog. Who has left them off their leads? Kamerdin arrives soon after and tells me his car has been serviced. The mechanics are two boys, one nine and the other ten.

We go all around Peshawar and start at the university. It's huge and the roads inside the complex are tranquil havens compared with the noise in the city centre. Kamerdin tells me he has three video games shops. These supplement the income he receives from NIFA. We have tea in Dean's Hotel and then go to Sarafa bazaar. I want to buy some paintings but one seller says he has a two hundred year old painting that costs thirty thousand rupees, about 1000 pounds. It's out of my price range. Kamerdin then takes me to some relations of his: all mujahideen. Many speak very good English. Questions come again. Who are the bravest fighters in the world? Which is the most beautiful city in Britain? One of the uncles works for the BBC in Peshawar and he reports to the Urdu service at Bush House, London.

When I get back, the door to my room has been locked. There is no key and there is great consternation because the lock has to be broken and after a few blows it is. I indicate by gesture and by imitating Safi's shouting that a new lock needs to be bought. It is and it costs me a fortune – eighteen rupees (54p)

Saturday August 13th

Kamerdin comes to take me to the museum. It is closed. I have to post some cards but first I have to master the intricacies of the post office. All the cards have to be put in envelopes and then addressed again. It costs seven rupees for a stamp and I find out later that a tailored suit costs two hundred rupees and one off the peg three hundred. How does that work? Afghan snuff is one rupee, a leather gun belt one hundred and fifty and sunglasses seventeen. We end up at the Pearl Continental hotel, the largest in Peshawar. The bill for tea for two and fancy ice cream is fifty three rupees, about £1.60. It's the most expensive place I've been to yet.

"The museum."

Sunday August 14th

Today is Independence Day in Pakistan and Kamerdin comes and takes me to the museum. It is quite interesting but the display itself is done poorly.

This afternoon the brigadier arrives. I think, at first, that he has a message for me from Safi: perhaps he is saying that I should get ready to go inside. Unfortunately it is not to be. Kamerdin will explain what *the craic* is.

Monday August 15th

Safi is still not back and I wonder if there is still time to go inside again. I would dearly love to. Abdul hammers on the door at 08.00 and "Chai, chai, eat, eat." I eat cheese, honey and nan and I take my anti-malaria tablets as I have done faithfully all the way through the trip. There is no paper today but I hear on the BBC World Service that Kunduz has fallen to the mujahideen.

I go to Sarafa bazaar again and buy two, small lapis lazuli horses, two brass figures and two Iranian paintings. One is of a lady sitting on a rug. On her right shoulder is a small wooden pole and at either end are two large ornamental pots. She wears much jewellery. The other is a colourful scene of thirteen men and two horses. The colours are rich: blues, reds and greys. In both pictures there is writing on the top and bottom. Persian?

Kamerdin comes tonight and says that he would have got all the goods for four hundred rupees less than I paid. I'm sure he's right. We talk about Islam and its varying interpretations, those mujahideen belonging to no party, how Pakistan is being given money by the Americans to help in Afghanistan but that only twenty five per cent is getting through to the seven parties and the refugees. We talk about Iraq and Iran and the prices in England. The boys are astounded when Kammerdin translates – £10 for a shirt, £12 a pair of jeans, £120 for a good camera.

Tuesday August 16th

Goats and sheep are in the garden chewing the grass and the dogs are going wild. I am told that Safi is due back early this evening. I hope so. I've had enough of looking around Peshawar for the moment. It's not that the boys are not looking after me. They are.

Safi returns at five forty five. There was a dispute near Khost between two tribes. He represents one of the tribes. The idea is to bring the two sides together to put their case to judges brought in from a different area. First, each party in the dispute give their weapons to the judges. The case is heard and the loosing faction must be punished in some way. Money, guns or sheep must be delivered to the winners in the dispute. Safi wins and chooses twelve sheep: one for each commander wronged. I don't know the reason for the dispute. Apparently it's a complicated story.

News must have spread of Safi's return because the buzzer goes. In come an old woman and two men. She is from Safi's own tribal area, Tagab in Kapisa province, and is crying and very emotional. One of the men has a son who was working with the Russians. He has been captured by some of Safi's group and the man has paid the woman to come and plead for the boy. She is no relation but might have some influence with Safi being from the same tribal area. In an adjoining room, the three visitors are shown some posters. They depict Russian atrocities during this war. They are told that the court will decide the boy's fate. They leave.

The post arrives. One of the letters is from Safi's wife. She wishes me well and hopes I am being looked after. I can't think of how anyone could be treated any better. Another comes from the Committee for a Free Afghanistan, Washington DC, indicating that funds are low but that the magazine *The Soldier of Fortune* would pay a return air fare for Safi and an examination by a cardiologist. I don't know anything about this and I try and impress on him that he should go and get checked out. He says he's too busy and I tell him to go for his wife's sake if not his own.

Wednesday August 17th

"The North West's Wild West."

We go to Dara Adam Khel about forty kilometres south of Peshawar. It is totally illegal for me to leave Peshawar and I am told that very few foreigners have been to Dara during the war. It has one main street and is the gun village of the North West Frontier Province. Nearly every shop is either making or selling guns and ammunition. You can buy machine guns, anti-aircraft guns, mausers, lugers, AK47s – any type of gun you want. If they don't have it they will make it. You test the guns outside in the street. We talk, and drink tea with goat's milk for forty five minutes in a shop that sells fountain pens and walking sticks. Guns. The fountain pens and the walking sticks are guns. It is unbelievable. I am severely tempted to buy a fountain pen gun but my career will be over if I am caught going back into the UK.

The boy in the shop goes to school but learns the trade from his father. He is an expert at ten. The family do not make all the parts. Each part is assembled elsewhere and then brought together. A Kalashnikov, the mujahideen's favourite gun, takes five days to copy and put together. The price here is a thousand dollars. Whether that's the price for me, a foreigner, I don't know. In fact we have come to Dara to get a serial number changed on a Kalashnikov. I think I know why but I don't ask. Usually if I'm meant to know I'm told. After the number has been changed or erased a leather craftsman makes a very skilful case for the gun.

"A Kalashnikov…takes five days to copy and put together."

Going Inside

I just cannot begin to understand things here. Safi just laughs and says that on one side of the army post near Dara it is illegal to have a gun and on the other side of the army post it is illegal NOT to have one. So, hustle, bustle, noise, firing in the street. It's the North West's Wild West.

We journey back and just like before there is no trouble at the army posts. Out of the blue I am asked if I want to go to Chitral, a Pakistani town at the foot of the Hindu Kush mountain range, and meet a friend of his – a prince. I am beyond being shocked. During my stay here there have been so many new experiences that I am now just living in the moment for the moment. I know that I will probably fly from Peshawar to Islamabad next Monday evening to catch my flight home on the Tuesday. The days are rushing by and my feelings are mixed about leaving. I miss Shirl but not much else. I haven't even been desperate for a pint.

It's quarter to nine and Safi says,

" Zia is dead. One bastard has gone."

The television is turned on and the newsreader is speaking very solemnly. President Zia's plane has crashed [12] and he and the many military staff accompanying him are dead. The report doesn't say where the plane crashed or if it was shot down. Zia's photograph is on the screen permanently. Safi leaves in the jeep to go to his office. Desdegira is sitting with me, shotgun at the ready and an ammunition belt on his shoulder. He looks a little shocked. Does he believe Zia was a good man?

Safi's instant reaction seemed almost ecstatic.

I can only get The Voice of America on the radio and it is the first item on the news. They say it's a plane crash and that the Vice President is taking over.

Thursday August 18th

Safi's brother in law arrives. He is the finance chief for NIFA and is extremely well educated: London, Paris and the USA. During the time of the king he was in charge of Radio Afghanistan. Widely travelled, marvellously cheerful and after Afghanistan he misses London the most. He taught Safi. I ask what that was like and he tells me a story. One day they go to the zoo and Safi rushes ahead of the teacher. They look at the animals and when they are leaving he says to Safi, "Stay. Stay here. This is where you belong." Safi has shown no respect by rushing ahead of the teacher. The concept of respect is hugely, hugely important in Afghan society.

As for teachers he has great respect for them. "A teacher teaches people to be human. The army teaches people to be animals." He has four sons and one daughter. Two are doctors, one a physiotherapist and a young son of fifteen who has won an eight thousand dollar annual scholarship to the Episcopalian college in Washington. After he leaves, Safi brings out his British Nationalization Forms and he asks me to help him fill them in. The form says he should not have left the UK for more than four hundred days in the last five years or ninety days in the last three years if married to a British citizen. His wife is a British citizen. Thus the five or three year residence requirements are totally up the creek. He should have applied in 1983 as he would have qualified for the five year requirement then.

He can't remember his wife's birthday, when they were married, their phone number in London, when Rohulla, his son, was born. However he does have his national insurance number.

I notice, on the forms, there is a "special circumstances" division in the Home Office relating to all of this and I urge him to write to them. He agrees. I write the letter which reads:

> *Dear Sir/Madam,*
>
> *Due to special circumstances, I am asking that my application for Naturalization as a British citizen be considered favourably.*
>
> *I arrived in Britain in December 1977 as a political refugee from Afghanistan.*

*In January 1978 I attended an interview in connection
with my continued stay in the United Kingdom.*

*From 1978-1983 I was both living and working
in High Wycombe, Bucks. I enclose photo copies
of documents that substantiate these claims.*

*In 1983, due to the Russian Invasion of Afghanistan,
I returned to my country to train the forces of the
mujahideen freedom fighters. Thus my continued
residence in Great Britain was necessarily interrupted,
though I have visited both my wife and son, who
are British passport holders, during this time.*

*I am at present a General in The National Islamic
Front of Afghanistan based in Peshawar.*

*Due to these special circumstances I am asking
that my application for Naturalization as a
British citizen be considered favourably.*

Yours faithfully etc...

I address it to the Home Office, Lunar House, Wellesley Rd, London
with Safi's reference number and Safi signs and dates it.

I say that he should also write to Lord Carrington, former foreign
secretary, or someone important. They may help his cause. Safi replies
that he could get an American passport very easily and I believe him.
The problem is that his wife and son are now British citizens and Safi
must obey his wife!

At five we walk along the Warsak road and come to a mansion. The
owner is a friend of Safi's and he owns much land, has a few businesses
and some schools. He shows me around his magnificent house and invites us for supper on Friday. I have to refuse as Kamerdin has already
invited me to his house then.

Tonight, after supper we talk about women, betrayal, honesty and,
according to Safi, the assassination of Zia. I am enjoying this visit for
so many reasons.

Going Inside

Friday August 18th

Today is like a Sunday in Britain as all the shops are closed and it is a day of rest. Safi complains of earache but has to attend a meeting at eight. He and the leaders of the seven mujahideen groups are going to Islamabad to attend the funeral of General Zia. We leave in the jeep and go to the meeting place of the seven. There is high security all around and the area seems hugely prosperous.

There is no way people can make this kind of money legally. I am informed guns and drugs are the answer. The jeep takes me back home.

In the afternoon, the buzzer goes and Safi's brother in law, the finance wizard of NIFA, and his son arrive again. The old man is very sprightly, intelligent and an avid fan of British culture and civilization. He says that though we have committed atrocities we brought with us many civilizing influences. The Russians have not learnt from British mistakes in Afghanistan.

He talks about literature, art, Eastern and Western civilizations.

"The supper at Kamerdin's house is memorable."

Going Inside

The supper at Kamerdin's house is memorable. There is beautiful rice, aubergine, home-made yoghurt, meat on and off the bone, and many other vegetables and fruit. I take some pictures. We talk of the role of women and in this Safi is a complete reactionary. We also compare and contrast life in the West and in Pakistan and Afghanistan. No women are present at the meal.

I now have Kamerdin's address and he wants me to find out about computer programming courses in Manchester and London. He also wants me to send *The American Book of Slang*.

Saturday August 20th

I get up today at 07.30 just in time to see Safi leave for the funeral. After breakfast I go to the Pakistan International Airlines office and book a ticket to Islamabad. My flight, from Peshawar, is at 17.00 on Tuesday so I will have some time to kill in the capital.

Most of the shops around the central square of Chowk Yadgar are closed but one place is open. It is very small and the man shows me all kinds of stone carvings. I try to indicate that I want paintings but I think anything on a stone is considered a painting. He says there is one at his house and will I go with him. I agree. We leave in a tuk-tuk and arrive in a narrow alley a few minutes later. We go up some stairs, enter a door and then a bedroom. Under the bed is a large "picture" in stone. It must weigh between eight and ten kilos. I look and say no thanks. We leave and he indicates that he wants to see a man nearby. This man speaks a little English and he says he sold a fine painting to "David's of London" a few months ago. I have never heard of them.

I must admit I am foolish going off into the dark, narrow alleys but I am safe and well. I just hope Desdegira is not doing his nut with me for being so long. I arrive back by tuk-tuk and the driver wants twenty. I say eight and he smiles and says okay.

Indeed, Desdegira goes nuts. It is my fault and I can't blame him. He would be in deep trouble if anything happened to me.

After lunch we all watch the funeral on the television and there are many tut-tut-tuts and shaking of heads. There are not tens of thousands there, as stated on the World Service, but hundreds of thousands. The scenes are quite amazing with large numbers of people on the tops of the minarets of the Faisal Mosque, a spectacular building financed by Saudi Arabia and finished only a few months ago.

This devotion to a man is a little frightening, almost, no not almost, it is – fanatical. The outward form of religion permeates much of this society.

Zia, presumably, has done much for Pakistan but Safi certainly doesn't want his type of fundamentalism in Afghanistan.

I go out to get some cigarettes, with Desdegira of course, and there are crowds of people watching Zia's funeral on a tiny black and white television set. On the way back there is a man with one leg and half a stump. He is beseeching people to give him some money – half in a

".We all watch the funeral on the television."

whimper, half in a scream. It is a terrible, terrible sound. I stop and give him two rupees. Desdegira says no and when I insist, he says one. I give him two.

Safi arrives at 19.45 with Abzel. His driver is here with him too and he salutes me and gives me a broad smile. The boys are obviously pleased to see everyone back. I say to Safi that both Abduls are gentle men. He gets confused as he says all the boys are gentlemen. That's how he has brought them up. He expects the four will return to their homes eventually but that Desdegira and Abzel will remain with him.

Safi then announces that we are going to his wealthy Pakistani friend for supper so it's down the Warsak road again.

The meal is out of this world; very spicy with garlic, chicken and so many kinds of curried vegetable. It is so unlike Afghan food. I must be careful. I have a little but am told to have more. "It is insulting not to have more," Safi says. I have more.

On the way out I slip and fall down a deep hole. Water is up to my knee. I have cut my foot and lost one of Safi's sandals. Back home I wash the cut, put on Savlon and then a plaster.

Going Inside

Sunday August 21st

After breakfast I take Paludrine and Nivaquine. These are the anti-malarial medicines I have been taking religiously during my visit. Within a few minutes I have to be sick and a few minutes after that I have to rush to the toilet again. Diarrhoea. I take two tablets for this immediately. I don't feel bad.

At nine we go to Peshawar. Safi needs to photocopy some documents that I am to send to Rohulla when I get home. Then it's the carpet shop and it's amazing.

"I am told to stop them when I like one."

"I choose two."

We sit down at one end and are given tea. A huge pile of rugs is at the other end stacked up high. Two men throw one rug down, wait a short time and then throw another down. I am told to stop them when I like one. After lengthy deliberation and with Safi's advice I choose two. One of them I am going to give to Safi as a present. I will hide it in the cupboard in the bedroom and then will tell him at the airport that I have left him a small gift. Otherwise he won't accept anything.

After the carpets we go to the cotton market. I have asked what I could get for the boys and new clothes is the answer. Altogether, for the material and the making of seven shirts and trousers it's one thousand and fifty rupees (£35). Amazing. Also I give Safi some money to buy sweets for the children at Jaji and a chicken for the old man at Meirzaka. I leave Desdegira my walking boots.

We return home and I need the toilet immediately and then again. I have a fever and I just lie on the bed waiting for the next attack. I have a little to eat this evening before going to bed at ten.

At 22.30, 23.30, 01.30, 03.30 it keeps coming and I am very groggy. I hardly sleep.

Going Inside

"The boys…with their guns."

At 08.30 I have a shower and then the paludrine with a cup of tea. Back they come. Then, as if by magic, the diarrhoea tablets start to work. I lie on the bed and drink green tea. I must drink to counter the dehydration. By dinnertime I am a little better.

To eat, I have one or two potatoes, a piece of bread and a few spoons of rice.

We leave Safi's at 16.00 and so I say goodbye to the boys and take a few pictures of them with their guns. I am so grateful to them all.

I am writing this in a restaurant at Islamabad airport. Flying from Peshawar is very quick, about forty five minutes and I now hope the diarrhoea has stopped. I am feeling much, much better.

The events of the last three weeks seem a little dreamlike but I want to record my impressions. Materially, there is no comparison between the majority of the people in the West and the majority of the people in Pakistan and Afghanistan. That is obvious. However, the virtues that the people have shown me in their everyday lives are much more important and mean much more than at home. The ability to sit and talk about meaningful ideas, the ability to show great hospitality and kindness even in poverty, the ability to make guests feel honoured and welcome and the ability to laugh when crying would be easier.

What else?

- To call a taxi or someone you make a kind of tutting sound.
- Always bargain for everything. There is no set price even when prices are shown on the object.
- The Afghan way is not to say please and thank you.
- If people come to your house they are automatically a guest and treated as such. This is important.
- Trust is a basic part of Afghan philosophy. Break the trust and you could be a dead man.
- The act of praying, whether here or in Britain, does not necessarily mean the person praying is good.
- In Safi's house you do what you want when you want. You want a drink, take it. You want to go to bed, you go. My house is your house. There are very few of the formalities and conventions that most UK people adhere to.
- The notion of respect is imperative.

Safi is a wily old fox and I love him. He has definite charisma, makes an impression and influences people. They look at him, pay attention and regard his words with almost a reverential air. It is a little frightening as often he looks stern and he shouts sometimes. But when I ask him about this, the shouting, it isn't like our kind of shouting. It's to make a point. His servants are devoted but not scared.

I have seen him upstaged only twice, both times by the intellectual, his brother in law. I have learned, here, not to agree with him on all matters. Some of his views are not mine.

He is a true friend and I am so glad to have met both him and his family.

Postscript

Saturday February 27th 1999

My wife, Shirley, and I went to see Safi and his wife in London. It was about two years since we had seen them. There had been telephone calls and a few letters but no direct, face to face contact. We arrived at 12.00 just as his wife was going out shopping. Safi was still in his pyjamas. We hugged both of them and went upstairs.

Safi explained what he believed happened after the Russians left Afghanistan (1988/1989) and the mujahideen took control of the country in 1992.

The Russians left in 1989 and the communist President of Afghanistan, Najibullah, held onto power until 1992. In 1992 Safi took a position in the Defence Ministry. His superior was Ahmad Shah Massoud, a very famous military commander in the Panjshir valley, North Afghanistan. Following the rise of the Taliban and their capture of Kabul, Massoud returned to armed opposition. Massoud was assassinated on September 9th 2001 – two days before the September 11th attacks on the USA.

Safi didn't stay long. He became extremely frustrated with the infighting between the various mujahideen groups. He lasted a few months in Kabul but nothing worked. He had fought the Russians and now the great prize should have been peace. It was not to be – the divisions were too great. Massoud and Hekmatyar could not agree on the way the country was going to be. The King was still in Rome.

He had tried to retrieve his property in Kabul, he had captured 200 Russian tanks months before the final Russian withdrawal and some fantastic treasure was unearthed in the orchard where I had seen the goat being killed at Rowd near Gardez.

All was in vain. So he went back to London to the security of his own home, his wife and son and where he gained naturalization.

In 1998 Safi had returned to Afghanistan with Nabi Misdak [13] and tried to convince Mullah Omar, the head of the Taliban, to hand over Osama bin Laden to foreign authorities. He was unsuccessful.

Interviewed by *Newsweek* in London, Safi said,

> *I told Omar, I don't know how Osama bin Laden will*
> *provide heaven to the Muslims of Afghanistan. But*
> *already here [Afghanistan] they are living in hell.*
> *In history, we have never been a terrorist people.*

Safi decided to write in Pushtu, his native language about the events that had happened in his country since the war began. He was highly critical of the main protagonists, including various mujahideen leaders and the Americans.

January 2001

Safi was erroneously named as the "Taliban representative in Europe" by the Security Council Committee on Afghanistan at the United Nations and listed. Being on a "Consolidated List" meant his assets were frozen and he was unable to travel.

Tuesday September 25th 2001

Safi was in Charring Cross hospital. He was awaiting an operation for bowel cancer. When I phoned the ward I was told he wasn't there, that he was outside having a smoke. When I did eventually speak to him he told me he had now retired from the fight. He was in good spirits and very pleased with his doctors.

When he spoke to Shirley he told her that he had finished with Afghanistan and repeated that he was now practising for Paradise.

His last words on the phone were, "Inshallah, I love you."

December 2004

The Security Council Committee "approves correction of information relating to Rahmatullah Safi." He was no longer on the list.

2005

Safi died on the 19th of November 2005.

Endnotes

1 A very famous man was at Jaji too. His name was Osama
bin Laden (1957-2011). In April 1987 Soviet Airborne
Troops (Spetnaz) attacked Jaji. Bin Laden and his
small force of Arab fighters fought alongside the Afghan
mujahideen. In August 1988 bin Laden founded al-Qaeda.

2 Heckmatyar, born in 1947, is a former Prime Minister
of Afghanistan. He met Margaret Thatcher in
Downing Street and was the recipient of the majority
of American aid during the war with Russia.

3 Zahir Khan (1914-2007) was the last king (Shah) of
Afghanistan. He returned to Afghanistan in 2002
and was given the title "Father of the Nation."

4 Pathan tribes inhabit southern and eastern Afghanistan
and western Pakistan. Their language is Pashto and
the vast majority are Sunni Muslims. They are the
largest and most influential ethnic group in Afghanistan
and follow Pashtunwali which is a traditional set of
rules relating to individual and group behaviour.

5 The KGB was the main security agency for the
Soviet Union until its break up in 1992. It then
became the FSB. The Russian President, Vladimir
Putin, was a KGB officer for sixteen years.

6 Khost is a city in eastern Afghanistan and has a
population of 160,000. The whole province has a million
people. It is 100 kilometres south east of Gardez.

Going Inside

7   Mohammad Najibullah (1947-1996) was born in
     Kabul but his ancestral home was at Mehlan, a small
     village between Said Karam and Gardez. He was
     President of Afghanistan from 1987 until 1992, when
     the mujahideen took over Kabul, and he took refuge
     in the United Nations headquarters in the city. When
     the Taliban took Kabul in 1996, he was shot and then
     strung up on a pole outside the Presidential palace.

8   This may refer to Andy Skrzypkowiak, a freelance
     news cameraman, who was murdered by
     followers of a fundamentalist mujahideen group
     near Antiwah, Nuristan, in October 1987.

9   Gailani, born in 1932, was an ethnic Pashtun. He founded
     The National Islamic Front of Afghanistan in 1979.
     This party supported the exiled king Zahir Khan.

10   Hesb-i-Islami is a mujahideen party led by Younis
     Khalis. Two prominent commanders associated with
     this party were Jalaluddin Haqqani and Abdul Haq.

11   Deans and Greens are famous hotels and meeting
     places in Peshawar. Deans was demolished in 2010.

12   A Pakistani general, Muhammad Zia-ul-Haq was
     the President of Pakistan from 1978 to 1988.

13   Misdaq is an author and journalist. He was the
     founder and head of the Pashto Section at the
     BBC World Service in the early nineteen eighties.
     As of 2016 he is the Media Affairs advisor to
     Ashraf Ghani the President of Afghanistan.

Going Inside